Editor
Eric Migliaccio

Managing Editor
Ina Massler Levin, M.A.

Cover Artist
Barb Lorseyedi

Art Coordinator
Kevin Barnes

Imaging
Craig Gunnell

Publisher
Mary D. Smith, M.S. Ed.

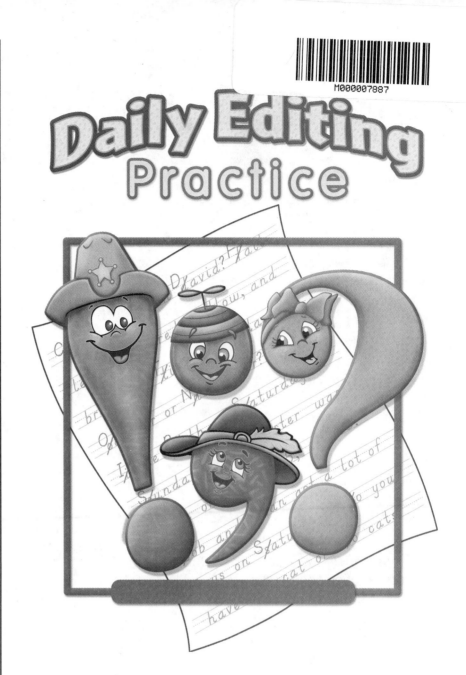

Daily Editing Practice

Author

Janelle Condra, M.A. Ed.

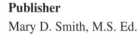

Teacher Created Resources, Inc.
6421 Industry Way
Westminster, CA 92683
www.teachercreated.com

ISBN-0-4206-3278-7
©2006 Teacher Created Resources, Inc.
Made in U.S.A.

Table of Contents

Introduction

The purpose of the *Daily Editing Practice* program is to introduce, review, and practice basic language concepts needed to develop proficient writing skills. This consistent and frequent guided practice promotes skill mastery that will carry over to other classroom writing assignments.

This resource is designed as a ready-to-use daily language program. It can be utilized in the form of a consumable workbook or as individual reproducible worksheets. It is meant to be used in a guided group lesson and consists mainly of sentences written incorrectly followed by blank lines provided for the students to rewrite the corrected sentence.

There are eight units with 20 passages per unit. Each unit provides daily practice for four weeks. Weekly assessments, as well as end-of-the-unit assessments, are included to check progress. All skills introduced in a unit are periodically reviewed throughout the following units to reinforce and master skills taught. A cumulative assessment of all skills presented in the book is also included. An overview of skills taught and reinforced is provided on page 5 ("Scope and Sequence Skills Chart"). A blank passage page is also included (page 144) for teachers who choose to write their own sentences. This may be done for additional practice with specific skills or to individualize sentences. Answer keys—provided at the end of each unit—can be torn out if the book is being used as a consumable workbook.

Skill Rules

At the beginning of Units 1–4, any new skill presented is included on a "Rules to Know" page. Using these rules as guides, short lessons can be provided as needed by the teacher when introducing a new skill. These rules are not meant to be taught all at once, but individually as they come up in the unit sentences. If the book is not being used as a consumable workbook, these rule pages can be copied and given to students when skills are introduced. Students can keep these pages together in a folder or booklet as their own individual language skills rule book, to be reviewed or referred to as needed. In addition to the rules pages, a copy of the explanation of editing marks (page 6) may also be beneficial for students to have in their folder. In Units 5–8, no new skills are presented. These units provide review and practice of skills previously taught.

Practice Sentences

Practice pages have a passage written for each day. Students use the sheet for the day, and the teacher writes the same passages on the board. The passage is read and the class, as a group, corrects it together. The teacher asks for correction ideas from the students and makes changes to the sentence or sentences written on the board as students come up with correct responses. For every correction, the reason for the correction is given, as well as how to make the needed change. Conventions of print in writing, such as correct letter formation and proper spacing, should also be emphasized.

Introduction
(cont.)

Practice Sentences (cont.)

As the teacher corrects each error on the board, the students also correct the same errors on their papers. When the passage has been corrected, the class goes over each change again while students check to make sure they have corrected all errors on their papers. Finally, as an individual assignment, the students independently rewrite the corrected sentence or sentences on the blank lines provided. The following is an example of how students make corrections to a sentence during a guided group lesson.

to our

my mother she went two are friend kims house on sunday

Assessment

There are three types of assessments provided in this program. Weekly assessments consist of an incorrectly written passage and are used to check progress on skills learned that week. The skill assessment at the end of each unit tests many of the skills learned or reviewed in that unit. The cumulative assessment includes a sample of all skills presented in the book. These assessments provide a way to evaluate student progress and determine the need for additional reinforcement to the class or individual students in specific skill areas.

On all of these assessments, <u>each word, group of numbers, and punctuation mark is awarded one point and is counted as either totally correct or totally incorrect.</u> The points possible represent the total number of words, groups of numbers, and punctuation marks in the passage. The number possible is indicated at the bottom of the page after each assessment. In the example above, the total points possible would be 13, counting one point for each of the 11 words and one point for each of the two punctuation marks.

to our

my mother she went two are friend kims house on sunday

Score: __13__ /13

Standards Alignment

State standards in the language arts/writing area for elementary grades emphasize conventions of print and editing written work using correct letter formation, spacing, grammar, punctuation, capitalization, and spelling. This is exactly what the *Daily Editing Practice* program provides. Teachers will be meeting standards requirements in this language-arts area while providing consistent and frequent practice leading to mastery and retention of needed skills for developing writers.

Scope & Sequence Skills Chart

• = Skill Introduced
+ = Skill Reinforced

	Units							
	1	2	3	4	5	6	7	8
Capitalization								
Beginning of a sentence	•	+	+	+	+	+	+	+
The word "I"	•	+	+	+	+	+	+	+
Proper nouns/initials	•	+	+	+	+	+	+	+
Days of the week/Months of the year	•	+	+	+	+	+	+	+
Name title	•	+	+	+	+	+	+	+
Holidays	•	+	+	+	+	+	+	+
Titles of books	•	+	+	+	+	+	+	+
Address	•	+	+	+	+	+	+	+
Titles of other works		•	+	+	+	+	+	+
First word in a quote		•	+	+	+	+	+	+
Letter greeting/closing			•	+	+	+	+	+
Relationship nouns			•	+	+	+	+	+
Outline				•	+	+	+	+
Punctuation								
Ending sentences	•	+	+	+	+	+	+	+
Abbreviations	•	+	+	+	+	+	+	+
Dates	•	+	+	+	+	+	+	+
Possessives	•	+	+	+	+	+	+	+
Series of words	•	+	+	+	+	+	+	+
Address	•	+	+	+	+	+	+	+
Contraction	•	+	+	+	+	+	+	+
Colon/time	•	+	+	+	+	+	+	+
Titles of books	•	+	+	+	+	+	+	+
Titles of other works		•	+	+	+	+	+	+
Quotations		•	+	+	+	+	+	+
Friendly letter			•	+	+	+	+	+
Compound sentence			•	+	+	+	+	+
Setting apart names				•	+	+	+	+
Single introductory words				•	+	+	+	+
Outline				•	+	+	+	+
Grammar & Usage								
Homophones	•	+	+	+	+	+	+	+
Plurals	•	+	+	+	+	+	+	+
Word order	•	+	+	+	+	+	+	+
Pronoun usage	•	+	+	+	+	+	+	+
Verb tenses		•	+	+	+	+	+	+
Misspelled/misused verbs		•	+	+	+	+	+	+
Subject/verb agreement		•	+	+	+	+	+	+
Irregular past tense verbs		•	+	+	+	+	+	+
Using a/an		•	+	+	+	+	+	+
Irregular plural nouns			•	+	+	+	+	+
Double negatives			•	+	+	+	+	+
Run-on sentence			•	+	+	+	+	+
Double subjects				•	+	+	+	+
Comparative/superlative endings				•	+	+	+	+

Editing Marks

The following is an explanation of each of the editing marks used in this book.

Add (letter, word, etc.)	∧	Underline	_____
Delete (letter, word, etc.)	ℐ	Capitalize	≡
Add (period, comma, etc.)	⊙	Change word	she / ~~her~~
Spelling Error	⬭	Add these marks where needed:	! ? , : ' " "

The box above contains the editing marks that are used in this book for the students' reference. The following are examples of how these editing marks are used when correcting errors in the language passages.

she read the book <u>america</u> ⟨two⟩ us on monday⊙ *(to)*

She read the book <u>America</u> to us on Monday.

my brother ~~he~~ likes play football⊙ *(ing)*

My brother likes playing football.

wasn't it ~~him~~ turn at 6 00? *(his)*

Wasn't it his turn at 6:00?

kim shouted, we ⟨one⟩ the game ! *(" won ")*

Kim shouted, "We won the game!"

Unit 1
Rules to Know

1. A *sentence* is a group off words that tells a complete thought. Capitalize the first word in a sentence.

   ➢ **<u>T</u>he dog is black.**

2. Capitalize the word "I."

   ➢ **Tom and <u>I</u> are friends.**

3. *Nouns* are words that name people, places, things, and ideas. Proper nouns name specific people, places, things, and ideas and begin with a capital letter. Capitalize the names of people, pets, specific places, etc.

   ➢ **I will play with <u>D</u>an and <u>P</u>uff.**

   ➢ **Is <u>P</u>ark <u>S</u>chool on <u>M</u>aple <u>S</u>treet?**

   ➢ **We went to <u>F</u>lorida on vacation.**

4. A *statement* is a sentence that tells something. Put a period at the end of a telling sentence. A *question* is a sentence that asks something. Put a question mark at the end of an asking sentence. An *exclamation* is a sentence that tells feeling. It ends with an exclamation mark. A *command* is a sentence that tells someone to do something. It ends with a period or an exclamation mark.

   ➢ **My house is white<u>.</u>**

   ➢ **Do you have a pet<u>?</u>**

   ➢ **We won the game<u>!</u>**

   ➢ **Please clean your room<u>.</u>**

   ➢ **Get out of the street<u>!</u>**

5. An *abbreviation* is a short form of a word. Capitalize name titles and put a period after ones that have been shortened into an abbreviation. Also capitalize and put a period after initials, which are letters used instead of a full name.

   Mister — Mr.   *Misses — Mrs.*   *Doctor — Dr.*

   ➢ **His friend is <u>Mr.</u> Brown.**

   ➢ **My teacher is <u>Mrs.</u> Lee.**

   ➢ **<u>Dr.</u> Rob is at the hospital.**

   ➢ **The author is <u>J.D.</u> Cummings.**

6. Capitalize the days of the week, months of the year, and holidays. Do not capitalize seasons of the year.

   ➢ **My birthday is on a Sunday in <u>M</u>ay.**

   ➢ **We have a big meal on <u>T</u>hanksgiving.**

   ➢ **My favorite season is <u>s</u>pring.**

7. A *possessive noun* shows ownership. Use an apostrophe and an *s* (*'s*) after a noun to show something belongs to one person or thing. To form the plural possessive of a plural noun that ends in *s*, add only an apostrophe. If the plural noun does not end in *s*, add an apostrophe and an *s*.

   ➢ **That is Beth<u>'s</u> room.**

   ➢ **Jess<u>'s</u> favorite food is ice cream.**

   ➢ **Both his brothers<u>'</u> bikes were blue.**

   ➢ **The new children<u>'s</u> library section is nice.**

8. Use a comma in a date to separate the day and year or to separate the day and month. Use a comma to separate a city and state.

   ➢ **She was born September 10<u>,</u> 2003.**

   ➢ **Was the play on Saturday, June 22<u>,</u> 2006?**

   ➢ **Do you live in Dallas<u>,</u> Texas?**

9. A series is a list of three or more items. Use a comma to separate three or more words or groups of words in a series.

   ➢ **Is your favorite food pizza<u>,</u> hamburger<u>,</u> or macaroni?**

   ➢ **At the zoo he saw a tiger<u>,</u> an elephant<u>,</u> and a bear.**

10. When writing the title of a book, underline the entire title and capitalize the first word, the last word, and each important word.

    ➢ **Have you read the book <u>Hansel and Gretel</u>?**

    ➢ **<u>Little Red Riding Hood</u> is my favorite book.**

11. A *pronoun* is a word that is used in place of a noun. Use the pronouns *we/us*, *she/he*, *her/him*, and *they/them* correctly.

    Use **we** — when you and others are doing something.

    Use **she/he/they** — when a person or group is doing something.

    Use **us** — when something happens to you and others.

    Use **her/him/them** — when something is happening to a person or a group.

    ➤ **<u>We</u> went to school.**

    ➤ **<u>He</u> is riding the bike.**

    ➤ **Sam gave <u>him</u> a ride.**

    ➤ **<u>They</u> gave the trophy to <u>us</u>.**

    ➤ **<u>She</u> will cook dinner for <u>them</u>.**

    ➤ **Bill took <u>her</u> to the movie.**

12. A *subject* tells who or what the sentence is about. In a sentence with more than one subject where the pronouns *I* or *me* are used, *I* or *me* is written last. (Hint: take out the second subject and read the sentence using only *I* or *me* to see which sounds correct.)

    Use *I* when you are doing something

    Use **me** when something happens to you

    ➤ **Tim and <u>I</u> went to the movie.**

    ➤ **She gave it to Bob and <u>me</u>.**

13. A *singular noun* names one person, idea, place, thing, or animal. A *plural noun* names more than one person, animal, place, thing, or idea. Add *s* to most nouns to make them plural. Add *es* to words that end in *s*, *ch*, *sh*, *x*, and *z*.

    ➤ **Where are the <u>dogs</u>? (*dog*)**

    ➤ **The <u>dishes</u> need to be washed. (*dish*)**

14. Nouns that end in the letter *y* have special rules for making plurals. If the word ends with a vowel followed by *y*, just add *s*. If the word ends with a consonant followed by *y*, change the *y* to *i* and add *es*.

    ➤ **I lost my <u>keys</u> yesterday. (*key*)**

    ➤ **She had three birthday <u>parties</u>. (*party*)**

15. Nouns that end in *f* or *fe* also have a special rule for making plurals. In most words, change the *f* to *v* and add *es*.

   ➤ **calf** becomes *calves*
   ➤ **knife** becomes *knives*
   ➤ **shelf** becomes *shelves*
   ➤ **elf** becomes *elves*

16. A *homophone* is a word that sounds the same as another word but has a different spelling or meaning. Learn to use homophones correctly. Here are some examples:

red / read	*knight / night*	*rode / road*
read / reed	*here / hear*	*eight / ate*
be / bee	*know / no*	*one / won*
knew / new	*sea / see*	*to / two / too*
four / for	*buy / by / bye*	*their / there / they're*
weak / week	*would / wood*	

17. A *colon* is used between the hour and minutes when writing the time of day.

   ➤ **We went to school at 8:00.**
   ➤ **In two hours it will be 3:30.**

18. A *contraction* is a word made by joining two words. When joining the words a letter or letters are left out. An apostrophe is put in the word at the spot where the letter or letters are missing.

   ➤ **We are going home.**   We're going home.
   ➤ **She did not see him.**   She didn't see him.
   ➤ **He will be there soon.**   He'll be there soon.

19. Write an address on three separate lines. Capitalize all names of people, as well as the names of streets, cities, and states. Capitalize an abbreviation for any type of street or road and put a period after it. Put a comma between the city and the state. Capitalize both letters in the state abbreviation, but do not put a period after it.

   ➤ **Mr. Joe Ross**
   16 Maple St.
   Minneapolis, MN 55382

did bills dog run away
on saturday

my friend and i went too
camp in boulder colorado

our school started on the first tuesday in september

me and ryans brother are in mr coopers class

Weekly Assessment

Directions: Use your editing marks to make corrections on the sentence(s) below. Then rewrite the sentence(s) on the lines provided.

me and my sister go too college in columbus ohio do you want two come and visit us my sisters friend will drive us back on sunday four christmas break

_____

_____

_____

_____

_____

_____

Score all words, group of numbers, or punctuation marks in these sentences as one point each, whether or not a correction is needed.

Score: _____ /35

him favorite book is
charlottes web by e b
white

are your teachers names
mrs green and miss
miller

those three girls cant go
with me and eric on
friday

is the play on saturday
at 7:00 or 7:30

Weekly Assessment

Directions: Use your editing marks to make corrections on the sentence(s) below. Then rewrite the sentence(s) on the lines provided.

miss cook red us a book called the mouse and the motorcycle on wednesday didnt you think it was funny im going too the library at 400 too check it out

_____

_____

_____

_____

_____

_____

Score all words, group of numbers, or punctuation marks in these sentences as one point each, whether or not a correction is needed.

Score: _____ /38

that boys brother was born on september 20 2005

her takes care of to dog five calfs and eleven bunnys on there farm

im so excited that my
team one first place on
sunday

---

mark adams
408 apple ave
richmond va 17932

Name: _____ Date: _____ Unit 1 - 15

Weekly Assessment

Directions: Use your editing marks to make corrections on the sentence(s) below. Then rewrite the sentence(s) on the lines provided.

my friends name is ali her
lives in oakland california
shes coming too visit on
thanksgiving im very
excited two sea her again

_____

_____

_____

_____

_____

_____

Score all words, group of numbers, or punctuation marks in these sentences as one point each, whether or not a correction is needed.

Score: _____ /31

me and my best friend
went too a concert at
300 last thursday
september 8

did them no the too girls
that were hurt on
tuesday

do you go two park
school in orlando florida

jim baker
39 rolling rd
duluth mn 56780

Weekly Assessment

Directions: Use your editing marks to make corrections on the sentence(s) below. Then rewrite the sentence(s) on the lines provided.

my brother was walking
with seth and i down
maple street we saw to boy
doing magic tricks those
boys tricks were awesome

_____

_____

_____

_____

_____

_____

*Score all words, group of numbers, or punctuation marks in these sentences
as one point each, whether or not a correction is needed.*

Score: _____ /27

Name: _____ Date: _____

Unit 1 Assessment

Directions: Use your editing marks to make corrections on the sentence(s) below. Then rewrite the sentence(s) on the lines provided.

did you no that flag day
was on tuesday june 14
2005 their was a parade
at 1000 down main street
i couldnt go because it was
also my sister erins birthday

_____

_____

_____

_____

_____

_____

Score all words, group of numbers, or punctuation marks in these sentences as one point each, whether or not a correction is needed.

Score: _____ /40

Unit 1
Answer Key

1. Did Bill's dog run away on Saturday?

2. My friend and I went to camp in Boulder, Colorado.

3. Our school started on the first Tuesday in September.

4. Ryan's brother and I are in Mr. Cooper's class.

5. My sister and I go to college in Columbus, Ohio. Do you want to come and visit us? My sister's friend will drive us back on Sunday for Christmas break.

6. His favorite book is <u>Charlotte's Web</u> by E. B. White.

7. Are your teachers' names Mrs. Green and Miss Miller?

8. Those three girls can't go with Eric and me on Friday.

9. Is the play on Saturday at 7:00 or 7:30?

10. Miss Cook read us a book called <u>The Mouse and the Motorcycle</u> on Wednesday. Didn't you think it was funny? I'm going to the library at 4:00 to check it out.

11. That boy's brother was born on September 20, 2005.

12. She takes care of two dogs, five calves, and eleven bunnies on their farm.

13. I'm so excited that my team won first place on Sunday!

14. Mark Adams
    409 Apple Ave.
    Richmond, VA 17932

15. My friend's name is Ali. She lives in Oakland, California. She's coming to visit on Thanksgiving. I'm very excited to see her again!

16. My best friend and I went to a concert at 3:00 last Thursday, September 8.

17. Did they know the two girls that were hurt on Tuesday?

18. Do you go to Park School in Orlando, Florida?

19. Jim Baker
    39 Rolling Rd.
    Duluth, MN 56780

20. My brother was walking with Seth and me down Maple Street. We saw two boys doing magic tricks. Those boys' tricks were awesome!

Unit 1 Assessment
<u>Answer Key</u>

did you ~~no~~ *know* that flag day was on tuesday,
june 14, 2005? ~~their~~ *there* was a parade at 10:00
down main street. i couldn't go because it
was also my sister erin's birthday.

Did you know that Flag Day was on Tuesday, June 14, 2005?

There was a parade at 10:00 down Main Street. I couldn't go

because it was also my sister Erin's birthday.

Unit 2
Rules to Know

1. The *subject* of a sentence tells who or what the sentence is about. When the subject is *singular*, an *-s* or *-es* is usually added to the verb except with the pronouns *I* or *you*. When the subject is *plural*, an *-s* is not added to the verb.

   ➤ **Ryan <u>runs</u> very fast.**
   ➤ **Eric and Bob <u>run</u> faster.**
   ➤ **Mom <u>fixes</u> lunch for us.**
   ➤ **You <u>run</u> on the track team.**
   ➤ **I do not <u>run</u> very fast.**
   ➤ **They <u>fix</u> lunch for us everyday.**

2. A *present tense verb* shows action that happens now. A *past tense verb* tells about an action that already happened. Add *-ed* to most verbs to form past tense. Besides *-s* or *-es*, the ending *-ing* can also be added to present tense verbs. If the verb has a single vowel and ends with a consonant, the last consonant is usually doubled before adding *-ed* or *-ing*. If the word ends with silent *e*, drop the final *e* before adding *-ed* or *-ing*.

   ➤ **Yesterday he <u>painted</u> the house.**
   ➤ **The rabbit <u>hopped</u> away.**
   ➤ **They <u>liked</u> their new school.**
   ➤ **The girl <u>is</u> jumping rope.**
   ➤ **The car <u>is</u> stopping here.**
   ➤ **The boy <u>is</u> riding his bike.**

3. If a verb ends with a consonant and *-y*, change the *y* to *i* and add *-es* to form a present tense verb. If a verb ends with a consonant and *-y*, change the *y* to *i* and add *-ed* to form a past tense verb.

   ➤ **The bird <u>flies</u> away. (*fly*)**
   ➤ **The girl <u>copied</u> the story into her journal. (*copy*)**

4. The past tense of some verbs is made by changing the spelling.

   ➤ **Last week my dog <u>ran</u> away. (*run*)**
   ➤ **We <u>bought</u> some milk at the store. (*buy*)**
   ➤ **He <u>drew</u> a picture in art class. (*draw*)**

5. *Helping verbs* are sometimes used with main action verbs. Some examples of helping verbs are *has*, *have*, *had*, *is*, *are*, *was*, *were*, and *will*. The words *saw* and *seen* tell about something in the past. Use *saw* without a helping verb, and use *seen* with a helping verb.

   ➤ **Yesterday I <u>saw</u> you at the mall.**
   ➤ **I have <u>seen</u> you there before.**

6. The verbs *am*, *are*, *is*, *was*, and *were* are forms of the word *be* and are not action words, instead they tell what someone or something is like.

   Use <u>*am*</u> with the word <u>*I*</u>.

   Use <u>*is*</u> and <u>*are*</u> when talking about what is happening now.

   Use <u>*was*</u> and <u>*were*</u> when talking about things that have already happened.

   Use <u>*is*</u> and <u>*was*</u> when talking about one person, animal, place, thing, or idea.

   Use <u>*are*</u> and <u>*were*</u> when talking about more than one person, animal, place, thing, or idea and with the word <u>*you*</u>.

   ➤ **I <u>am</u> six years old.**
   ➤ **Jim <u>is</u> seven years old.**
   ➤ **Kate and Nate <u>are</u> eight.**
   ➤ **You <u>are</u> six years old.**
   ➤ **Last year Jim <u>was</u> six.**
   ➤ **They <u>were</u> seven last year.**

7. Use *doesn't* with singular nouns meaning one person, animal, place, thing, or idea. Use *don't* with plural nouns meaning more than one person, animal, place, thing, or idea and with *I*, *you*, *we*, and *they*.

   ➤ **Joe <u>doesn't</u> like to play tag.**
   ➤ **That dog <u>doesn't</u> belong to me.**
   ➤ **I <u>don't</u> think he is ready yet.**
   ➤ **The new kittens <u>don't</u> have names.**

8. Use the helping verb *has* with one subject. Use the helping verb *have* with more than one subject and with the words *I* and *you*.

   ➤ **The dog <u>has</u> a bone.**
   ➤ **The boys <u>have</u> the ball.**
   ➤ **I <u>have</u> a sister.**
   ➤ **You <u>have</u> a brother.**

9. Do not use the word *ain't* or spell verbs incorrectly, as they are often mispronounced.

   ➤ **We <u>ain't</u> going.**   **We <u>are not</u> going.**
   ➤ **We <u>wanna</u> leave.**   **We <u>want to</u> leave.**
   ➤ **Are you <u>gonna</u> go?**   **Are you <u>going to</u> go?**
   ➤ **<u>Gimme</u> that paper.**   **<u>Give me</u> that paper.**

10. Capitalize the first word, last word, and each important word in titles of books, stories, poems, songs, movies, and television shows. When writing these titles in a sentence, underline (or *italicize*) the titles of books, movies, plays, music collections, and television shows. Use quotation marks around the titles of stories, poems, and songs. If the title comes at the end of the sentence, put the final quotation mark after the period.

> ➤ **My favorite television show is <u>American Heroes</u>.**

> ➤ **I like the song "Somewhere Over the Rainbow."**

> ➤ **Yesterday we read the poem "The Night Before Christmas."**

> ➤ **<u>Holes</u> is my favorite book.**

11. Use *a* or *an* before *singular nouns* (words meaning one person, place, thing, or animal). Use *a* before words that begin with a consonant sound. Use *an* before words beginning with a vowel or vowel sound.

> ➤ **He had <u>a</u> bowl of cereal for breakfast.**

> ➤ **She had <u>an</u> egg for breakfast.**

> ➤ **She ate <u>an</u> hour before he did.**

12. A quotation shows the speaker's exact words. Use quotation marks at the beginning and ending of a quotation to show where the speaker started and stopped talking. Begin a quotation with a capital letter. When writing a quotation, put the punctuation marks inside the quotation marks.

> ➤ **<u>"</u>Today we are going to the zoo,<u>"</u> said Bill.**

> ➤ **Mary asked, <u>"</u>Can we go with you?<u>"</u>**

13. Use the correct punctuation to separate a quotation from the rest of the sentence. In a telling sentence, use a comma between the quotation and the rest of the sentence and end the sentence with a period.

> ➤ **Dad said, "It is raining."**

> ➤ **"It is raining," said Dad.**

14. In an *asking sentence*, use a question mark after the quotation. If the quotation is before the speaker's name, put a period at the end of the sentence. If the speaker's name is before the quotation, separate the quotation with a comma.

➤ **"Where are we going?" asked Jane.**

➤ **Jane asked, "Where are we going?"**

15. In an *exclamation,* use an exclamation mark at the end of the quotation. If the quotation is before the speaker's name, put a period at the end of the sentence. If the speaker's name is before the quotation, separate the quotation with a comma.

➤ **"That house is on fire!" shouted the man.**

➤ **The man shouted, "That house is on fire!"**

16. Be careful not to confuse these words: *are* and *our*, *you're* and *your*, *it's* and *its*, *then* and *than*.

are is a verb

our means something belongs to us

you're is the contraction for "you are"

your is a pronoun that shows ownership

it's is a contraction for "it is" or "it has" (use an apostrophe in a contraction)

its is a possessive pronoun that shows ownership (do not use an apostrophe)

then is used when telling what happens next

than is used when comparing things

➤ **<u>Are</u> you coming to <u>our</u> house today?**

➤ **<u>You're</u> the youngest member of <u>your</u> family.**

➤ **<u>It's</u> time to give the dog <u>its</u> bath.**

➤ **<u>It's</u> been a long time since I have seen you.**

➤ **<u>Then</u> we went on a long walk.**

➤ **She is older <u>than</u> her sister.**

17. A name can be made into a contraction as well as a possessive by adding *'s*. The *'s* can mean "is" or "has," depending on the sentence.

➤ **Mary<u>'s</u> going to go with us tomorrow.**

➤ **Mark<u>'s</u> gone to the park many times.**

him favorite fall book is
the big pumpkin

---

thats way to big two fit
in hear shouted kim

me and pam buyed too
pumpkins four
halloween said meg

do you like red yellow or
orange leaves asked mr
clark

Name: _____ Date: _____

Weekly Assessment

Directions: Use your editing marks to make corrections on the sentence(s) below. Then rewrite the sentence(s) on the lines provided.

i runned in a long race last wednesday at 100 said ben didnt you get tired asked jan i also likes runing in races said beth

_____

_____

_____

_____

_____

_____

Score all words, group of numbers, or punctuation marks in these sentences as one point each, whether or not a correction is needed.

Score: _____ /40

does you likes the song angel the best

_____

_____

_____

_____

_____

_____

im gonna have a apple and a orange four a snack

_____

_____

_____

_____

_____

all the neighbors houses
on pine street was
painted white

susan russell
47 spruce st
madison wisconsin 54307

Weekly Assessment

Directions: Use your editing marks to make corrections on the sentence(s) below. Then rewrite the sentence(s) on the lines provided.

yesterday i stoped at the library and seen a book called classic fairy tails i red the story called the princess and the pea

_____

_____

_____

_____

_____

_____

Score all words, group of numbers, or punctuation marks in these sentences as one point each, whether or not a correction is needed.

Score: _____ /29

miss davis asked what
are you gonna bee for
halloween

doesnt you think the
television show called
aliens is really scary

is both the halloween partys on monday october 31

my friends name is a j carson said jerry

Weekly Assessment

Directions: Use your editing marks to make corrections on the sentence(s) below. Then rewrite the sentence(s) on the lines provided.

my brother bills gonna visit are cousin in reno nevada in november he flys out of minneapolis at 500 and gets their at 800 him already buyed a ticket

_____

_____

_____

_____

_____

Score all words, group of numbers, or punctuation marks in these sentences as one point each, whether or not a correction is needed.

Score: _____ /36

watch out four that car yelled nates brother

your are favorite babysitter the twins said two alissa

the coach said its gonna start write away

jill jackson
17 ocean ave
san francisco ca 97601

Name: _____   Date: _____

Weekly Assessment

Directions: Use your editing marks to make corrections on the sentence(s) below. Then rewrite the sentence(s) on the lines provided.

jake and bill was siting
on the beach four a hour
than them seen a big fish
out in the see aint that a
whale asked bill

_____

_____

_____

_____

_____

_____

*Score all words, group of numbers, or punctuation marks in these sentences
as one point each, whether or not a correction is needed.*

Score: _____ /33

Unit 2 Assessment

Directions: Use your editing marks to make corrections on the sentence(s) below. Then rewrite the sentence(s) on the lines provided.

kate red the poem rainbows on tuesday in english class then her writed her own poem called a eagle kates teacher liked it i thinked it was vary good said mrs mitchell

_____

_____

_____

_____

_____

Score all words, group of numbers, or punctuation marks in these sentences as one point each, whether or not a correction is needed.

Score: _____ /45

Unit 2
Answer key

1. His favorite fall book is <u>The Big Pumpkin</u>.

2. "That's way too big to fit in here!" shouted Kim.

3. "Pam and I bought two pumpkins for Halloween," said Meg.

4. "Do you like red, yellow, or orange leaves?" asked Mr. Clark.

5. "I ran in a long race last Wednesday at 1:00," said Ben. "Didn't you get tired?" asked Jan. "I also like running in races," said Beth.

6. Do you like the song "Angel" the best?

7. I'm going to have an apple and an orange for a snack.

8. All the neighbors' houses on Pine Street were painted white.

9. Susan Russell
   47 Spruce Street
   Madison, Wisconsin 54307

10. Yesterday I stopped at the library and saw a book called <u>Classic Fairy Tales</u>. I read the story called "The Princess and the Pea."

11. Miss Davis asked, "What are you going to be for Halloween?"

12. Don't you think the television show called <u>Aliens</u> is really scary?

13. Are both Halloween parties on Monday, October 31?

14. "My friend's name is A.J. Carson," said Jerry.

15. My brother Bill's going to visit our cousin in Reno, Nevada, in November. He flies out of Minneapolis at 5:00 and gets there at 8:00. He already bought a ticket.

16. "Watch out for that car!" yelled Nate's brother.

17. "You're our favorite babysitter," the twins said to Alissa.

18. The coach said, "It's going to start right away."

19. Jill Jackson
    17 Ocean Ave.
    San Francisco, CA 97601

20. Jake and Bill were sitting on the beach for an hour. Then they saw a big fish out in the sea. "Isn't that a whale?" asked Bill.

Unit 2 Assessment
Answer Key

kate ~~red~~ *read* the poem "rainbows" on tuesday in english class. then ~~her~~ *she* ~~writed~~ *wrote* her own poem called "~~An~~ *a* eagle." kate's teacher liked it. "~~i~~ ~~thinked~~ *thought* it was ~~vary~~ *very* good," said mrs. mitchell.

Kat'e read the poem "Rainbows" on Tuesday in English class.

Then she wrote her own poem called "An Eagle." Kate's teacher

liked it. "I thought it was very good," said Mrs. Mitchell.

Unit 3
Rules to Know

1. Capitalize a relationship word used in place of a name if no word is used before it such as *my*, *your*, *their*, etc. To help determine if the relationship word should be capitalized, try substituting a name for the word. If the sentence makes sense, the word is being used in place of a name and should be capitalized.

   ➤ **Did <u>D</u>ad want to go with us?**   **My <u>d</u>ad wants to go with us.**

   ➤ **He thought <u>M</u>om was nice.**   **Your <u>m</u>om is nice.**

2. Some nouns change their spelling instead of adding *s* or *es* to mean more than one. A few nouns can mean either one or more with the same spelling. Examples of these irregular plural nouns are the following:

man / men	**woman / women**
child / children	**mouse / mice**
foot / feet	**tooth / teeth**
sheep / sheep	**deer / deer**

3. A *negative* is a word like *no*, *not*, *none*, or *never*. A contraction with the word *not* is also a negative. Do not use two negatives together in a sentence.

   ➤ **He doesn't have <u>no</u> money.**   **He doesn't have <u>any</u> money. (*correct*)**

   ➤ **She never had <u>no</u> lunch.**   **She never had <u>any</u> lunch. (*correct*)**

   ➤ **Can't you see <u>nothing</u>?**   **Can't you see <u>anything</u>? (*correct*)**

4. A *run-on sentence* has two complete thoughts that run into each other. Run-on sentences can be corrected by separating the thoughts. If the ideas in the two parts are separate thoughts, divide them into two sentences with a period.

   ➤ **Today it is rainy tomorrow is Saturday. (*incorrect*)**

   ➤ **Today it is rainy<u>.</u> Tomorrow is Saturday. (*correct*)**

5. If the two ideas in a run-on sentence go together by having something in common, make a *compound sentence* out of the two thoughts. A compound sentence is made by combining two short sentences into one longer one. The two sentences are joined with a comma and a connecting word such as *and*, *but*, *yet*, or *while*.

   ➤ **The girls go to West School their favorite subject is math. (*incorrect*)**

   ➤ **The girls go to West School<u>, and</u> their favorite subject is math. (*correct*)**

   ➤ **The boys wanted to play ball they couldn't find the field. (*incorrect*)**

   ➤ **The boys wanted to play ball<u>, but</u> they couldn't find the field. (*correct*)**

6. A friendly letter has five parts:

   1. heading

   2. greeting

   3. body

   4. closing

   5. signature

7. The <u>heading</u> contains the sender's address and the date. When writing an address, capitalize the names of streets, cities, and states. Write the street address on a separate line from the city and state. Capitalize an abbreviation for any type of street or road and put a period after it. Put a comma between the city and the state. Capitalize both letters in the state abbreviation, but do not put a period after it. Put a comma in the date between the day and the year.

   ➢ **9684 Sunset Lane**
   Des Moines, IA 50321
   December 5, 2004

8. The *greeting* of a letter greets the person you are writing to. Capitalize the first word of the greeting in a letter. Put a comma after the greeting in a friendly letter.

   ➢ **Dear Bob,**

   ➢ **Hello Jill,**

9. The way you end a letter is called the *closing*. Capitalize the first word of the closing in a letter and put a comma after it.

   ➢ **Your friend,**

   ➢ **Sincerely yours,**

10. The main part of a letter is called the *body*. Indent the first word of the body of a friendly letter by moving the first word a little to the right.

    ➢ **Dear Bob,**

      How are you? Did you get a new bike on Saturday? Come and visit me soon!

                    Your friend,

                    Dan

robert carryed too big boxs
two the house but it was
locked

---

kelly asked is mom
gonna go shoping on
saturday

dear amy you are my
best friend your friend
jill

mary asked will
thanksgiving bee on
thursday friday or
saturday

Weekly Assessment

Directions: Use your editing marks to make corrections on the sentence(s) below. Then rewrite the sentence(s) on the lines provided.

my sister like too read her
like the book turkey time
buy jane robbins sometimes
mom read it two her but
last weak her red it buy
herself

_____

_____

_____

_____

_____

*Score all words, group of numbers, or punctuation marks in these sentences
as one point each, whether or not a correction is needed.*

Score: _____ /33

did you no i seen real
turkies on bills farm

jeffs to dog's runned
away last friday said
dad

that womens name is
betty she is are neighbor

me and uncle jim likes
too play baseball at ford
park

Weekly Assessment

Directions: Use your editing marks to make corrections on the sentence(s) below. Then rewrite the sentence(s) on the lines provided.

416 spruce st toledo oh
64731 november 10 2006
dear molly will you bee
comeing too visit on
thanksgiving im hopeing you
will your friend nancy

_____

_____

_____

_____

_____

_____

_____

Score: _____ /34

my favorite poem is fall
by b j white

grandma and grandpa
are comeing too are
house four thanksgiving

those to childs cant go slideing down the hill with us

dont you got no candy left asked erin

Weekly Assessment

Directions: Use your editing marks to make corrections on the sentence(s) below. Then rewrite the sentence(s) on the lines provided.

me and tim wanna go too the movie but i dont got no money we will have two go too the 700 movie next weak at the showtime theater

_____

_____

_____

_____

_____

_____

Score all words, group of numbers, or punctuation marks in these sentences as one point each, whether or not a correction is needed.

Score: _____ /34

did you put a carrot a onion and a pepper in the soup

will thanksgiving bee on thursday november 24

those to mouses are gray
once we catched a mouse

jerrys two cat's are
named benny and penny

Weekly Assessment

Directions: Use your editing marks to make corrections on the sentence(s) below. Then rewrite the sentence(s) on the lines provided.

700 meadow drive detrioit mi 69423 november 20 2006 dear grandma i cant wait too sea you again im looking forward too you're delicious pumpkin pie with love nate

Score: _____ /37

Name: _____ Date: _____

Unit 3 Assessment

Directions: Use your editing marks to make corrections on the sentence(s) below. Then rewrite the sentence(s) on the lines provided.

today mom and dad is comeing
too my brothers baseball game
him is the pitcher and him is
vary good grandpa dont got no
time too come all the mans and
womans sits on the bleachers

_____

_____

_____

_____

_____

_____

*Score all words, group of numbers, or punctuation marks in these sentences
as one point each, whether or not a correction is needed.*

Score: _____ /42

Unit 3
Answer Key

1. Robert carried two big boxes to the house, but it was locked.

2. Kelly asked, "Is Mom going to go shopping on Saturday?"

3. Dear Amy,
   > You are my best friend.
   >> Your friend,
   >> Jill

4. Mary asked, "Will Thanksgiving be on Thursday, Friday, or Saturday?"

5. My sister likes to read. She likes the book <u>Turkey Time</u> by Jane Robbins. Sometimes Mom reads it to her, but last week she read it by herself.

6. Did you know I saw real turkeys on Bill's farm?

7. "Jeff's two dogs ran away last Friday," said Dad.

8. That woman's name is Betty, and she is our neighbor.

9. Uncle Jim and I like to play baseball at Ford Park.

10.
   > 416 Spruce St.
   > Toledo, OH 64731
   > November 10, 2006

   Dear Molly,
   > Will you be coming to visit on Thanksgiving? I'm hoping you will.
   >> Your friend,
   >> Nancy

11. My favorite poem is "Fall" by B.J. White.

12. Grandma and Grandpa are coming to our house for Thanksgiving.

13. Those two children can't go sliding down the hill with us.

14. "Don't you have any candy left?" asked Erin.

15. Tim and I want to go to the movie, but I don't have any money. We will have to go to the 7:00 movie next week at the Showtime Theater.

16. Did you put a carrot, an onion, and a pepper in the soup?

17. Will Thanksgiving be on Thursday, November 24?

18. Those two mice are gray. Once we caught a mouse.

19. Jerry's two cats are named Benny and Penny.

20.
> 700 Meadow Drive
> Detriot, MI 69423
> November 20, 2006

Dear Grandma,

　I can't wait to see you again! I'm looking forward to your delicious pumpkin pie.

> With love,
> Nate

Unit 3 Assessment

Answer Key

today mom and dad are~~is~~ com~~i~~ng (too) my brother's baseball game. He~~him~~ is the pitcher, and he~~him~~ is very (vary) good. grandpa doesn't~~dont~~ have~~got~~ any~~no~~ time (too) come. all the men~~mans~~ and women~~womans~~ sits on the bleachers.

Today, Mom and Dad are coming to my brother's baseball game.

He is the pitcher, and he is very good. Grandpa doesn't have any

time to come. All the men and women sit on the bleachers.

Unit 4
Rules to Know

1. The *subject* of a sentence tells who the sentence is about. A noun or a pronoun can be the subject of a sentence. Do not use both a noun and a pronoun to mean the same person or thing in a sentence.

   ➤ **<u>Tom he</u> came to my house.**   **<u>Tom</u> came to my house. (*correct*)**

   ➤ **The <u>girl she</u> went skating.**   **<u>The girl</u> went skating. (*correct*)**

   ➤ **<u>Jill and I we</u> like to play.**   **<u>Jill and I</u> like to play (*correct*)**

2. *An adjective* is a word that describes a noun or a pronoun. Add *er* to most adjectives to compare two people, places, things, or animals. Add *est* to compare more than two.

   ➤ **He is <u>taller</u> than his brother.**

   ➤ **He is the <u>tallest</u> student in the class.**

3. Use a comma after "yes" or "no" at the beginning of a sentence.

   ➤ **Are you Jan's sister?**   **<u>Yes,</u> I am her sister.**

   ➤ **Do you go to Valley School?**   **<u>No,</u> I go to Lake School.**

4. Use a comma to separate single introductory words at the beginning of a sentence.

   ➤ **<u>Wow,</u> it's hot outside today!**

   ➤ **<u>Oh,</u> I almost forgot the party.**

5. Usually a comma is used to set off the name of a person being directly addressed or described in a sentence.

   ➤ **<u>Bill,</u> are you going to the park today?**

   ➤ **Did you like the park<u>, Bill?</u>**

   ➤ **<u>Mrs. White,</u> our neighbor, is really nice.**

   ➤ **My dad<u>, John,</u> is the soccer coach.**

6. Use a comma to set off the word "too" when meaning "also."

   ➤ **My sister wanted to <u>go, too</u>.**

   ➤ **I want another turn<u>, too</u>.**

7. An *outline* is a way of organizing ideas. It can be made up of main topics, subtopics, and details. Follow these rules when writing an outline:

➢ An outline has a title that describes the subject. Capitalize the first word, the last word, and each important word in a title.

➢ Main topics are the most important ideas. Capitalize the first letter of each main topic and use Roman numerals with periods (I., II., etc.) when listing them.

➢ Subtopics give more information about the main topic. Indent the subtopics under the main topics. Capitalize the first letter of each subtopic and use capital letters starting with A and periods (A., B., etc.) when listing them.

➢ Details give more information about the subtopic. Indent the details under the subtopics. Capitalize the first letter of each detail and use numbers and periods (1., 2., etc.) when listing them.

Maple Trees

I. Appearance
   A. Leaves
      1. Have 3 to 5 sections
      2. Turn colors in fall

   B. Trunks
      1. Are 1 to 2 feet around
      2. Have gray or brown bark

II. Use
   A. Food
      1. Maple syrup

   B. In homes
      1. Furniture
      2. Firewood for heating

Name: _____ Date: _____

that boy he is hurt to
shouted chris

_____

_____

_____

_____

_____

_____

Name: _____ Date: _____

hi my name is beth
conners said my sisters
friend

_____

_____

_____

_____

my teacher mrs hanson
red us a book called its
fall

is you tallest than you're
brother kasey asked

Weekly Assessment

Directions: Use your editing marks to make corrections on the sentence(s) below. Then rewrite the sentence(s) on the lines provided.

do you wanna go too the mall said my sister jan yes when can us leave i asked my friend amy is meeting us their at 300 said jan

_____

_____

_____

_____

_____

_____

Score all words, group of numbers, or punctuation marks in these sentences as one point each, whether or not a correction is needed.

Score: _____ /46

that dogs tail is the
longer of all said ken

dont dads friend dr
brown live buy us no
more

my mom she drived us
two the movie on friday
said tony

tuesday knight their
was too foxs three wolfs
and a owl in are yard

Weekly Assessment

Directions: Make an outline. (Title) types of animals (Main topics) mammals, reptiles (Subtopics) dogs, snakes (Details) beagle, poodle, cobra, boa constrictor.

_____

_____

_____

_____

_____

_____

_____

_____

_____

_____

_____

*Score all words, group of numbers, or punctuation marks in these sentences
as one point each, whether or not a correction is needed.*

Score: _____ /28

nancys party will bee on
thursday december 24
at 700

robert did you sea the
show a jolly snowman on
television last knight

me and aunt sue goed
christmas shoping and
we buyed three gift

us seen some cows and
ponys at grandpas house

Weekly Assessment

Directions: Use your editing marks to make corrections on the sentence(s) below. Then rewrite the sentence(s) on the lines provided.

45 arrow hwy hollywood ca
97251 december 15 2006
dear uncle john i hope your
having fun in colorado
sea you on christmas your
nephew eric

_____

_____

_____

_____

_____

_____

*Score all words, group of numbers, or punctuation marks in these sentences
as one point each, whether or not a correction is needed.*

Score: _____ /33

ali bennet
206 maple st
new york city ny 26155

the childrens dentist dr
davis cleaned there
tooths on wednesday

did him by a christmas
tree yet my favorite type
of pine tree is spruce

merry christmas too all
and two all a good knight
shouted santa claus

Weekly Assessment

Directions: Make an outline. Add one more subtopic of your own to each main topic. (Title) transportation (Main topics) ground, air, water (Subtopics) car, airplane, boat.

_____

_____

_____

_____

_____

_____

_____

_____

_____

_____

_____

_____

Score all words, group of numbers, or punctuation marks in these sentences as one point each, whether or not a correction is needed.

Score: _____ /28

Unit 4 Assessment

Directions: Use your editing marks to make corrections on the sentence(s) below. Then rewrite the sentence(s) on the lines provided.

on christmas my dad he dress
up as santa claus my friend
bob comed over two my house
jim comed over to wow you're
dad is the fatter santa i have
ever saw said jim

_____

_____

_____

_____

_____

_____

*Score all words, group of numbers, or punctuation marks in these sentences
as one point each, whether or not a correction is needed.*

Score: _____ /46

1. "That boy is hurt, too!" shouted Chris.

2. "Hi, my name is Beth Conners," said my sister's friend.

3. My teacher, Mrs. Hanson, read us a book called <u>It's Fall</u>.

4. "Are you taller than your brother?" Kasey asked.

5. "Do you want to go to the mall?" said my sister, Jan. "Yes, when can we leave?" I asked. "My friend, Amy, is meeting us there at 3:00," said Jan.

6. "That dog's tail is the longest of all," said Ken.

7. Doesn't Dad's friend, Dr. Brown, live by us anymore?

8. "My mom drove us to the movie on Friday," said Tony.

9. Tuesday night there were two foxes, three wolves, and an owl in our yard.

10.
Types of Animals
I. Mammals

    A. dogs

        1. Beagle

        2. Poodle

II. Reptiles

    A. Snakes

        1. Cobra

        2. Boa Constrictor

11. Nancy's party will be on Thursday, December 24, at 7:00.

12. Robert, did you see the show <u>A Jolly Snowman</u> on television last night?

13. Aunt Sue and I went Christmas shopping, and we bought three gifts.

14. We saw some cows and ponies at Grandpa's house.

15.
> 45 Arrow Hwy.
> Hollywood, CA 97251
> December 15, 2006

Dear Uncle John,

    I hope you're having fun in Colorado. See you on Christmas!

> Your nephew,
> Eric

16. Ali Bennet
    206 Maple St.
    New York City, NY 26155

17. The children's dentist, Dr. Davis, cleaned their teeth on Wednesday.

18. Did he buy a Christmas tree yet? My favorite type of pine tree is spruce.

19. "Merry Christmas to all, and to all a good night!" shouted Santa Claus.

20.   **Transportation**

   I. Ground
      A. Car
      B. (answers will vary)
   II. Air
      A. Airplaine
      B. (answers will vary)
   III. Water
      A. Boat
      B. (answers will vary)

Unit 4 Assessment

<u>Answer Key</u>

on christmas my dad ~~he~~ dress^ed up as santa claus.
my friend, bob, ~~comed~~ came over (two)→to my house. jim
~~comed~~ came over, (to)→too. "wow, ~~you're~~ your dad is the ~~fatter~~ fattest
santa i have ever ~~saw~~ seen!" said jim.

On Christmas my dad dressed up as Santa Claus. My friend, Bob, came over to my house. Jim came over, too. "Wow, your dad is the fattest Santa I have ever seen!" said Jim.

the teacher said happy knew year everyone

is you oldest then you're brother asked are neighbor mr smith

us went on vacation two
daytona florida in
december

dont you likes too build
lots of snowmans in the
winter asked james

Weekly Assessment

Directions: Use your editing marks to make corrections on the sentence(s) below. Then rewrite the sentence(s) on the lines provided.

me and my family was gonna
go too a play my sister she
takes acting lessons and she
is in the play us needs too
leave in a hour two get their
buy 600 shouted dad

_____

_____

_____

_____

_____

Score all words, group of numbers, or punctuation marks in these sentences as one point each, whether or not a correction is needed.

Score: _____ /44

emily why dont you never
come swiming with us no
more

wintertime fun is a
great book i go too the
library every saturday
two check out books

sally drawed a picture
of all her puppys and
kittys

franks favorite song is
america by r w fields

Weekly Assessment

Directions: Make an outline. (Title) my garden (Main topics) food, flowers, (Subtopics) fruits, vegetables, annuals, perennials (Details) strawberries, corn, sunflowers, tulips

_____

_____

_____

_____

_____

_____

_____

_____

_____

_____

_____

_____

*Score all words, group of numbers, or punctuation marks in these sentences
as one point each, whether or not a correction is needed.*

Score: _____ /32

yesterday mom play golf
tennis and basketball
with i and kim

no i didnt catched a fish
all day shouted Zach

my dad he flys airplanes
just like his best friend
jake

i made three wishes
when i blowed out my
birthday candles

Weekly Assessment

Directions: Use your editing marks to make corrections on the sentence(s) below. Then rewrite the sentence(s) on the lines provided.

2020 greenview ave atlanta ga 72947 january 15, 2006 dear rod im having fun in san francisco us goed too a zoo a ocean beach and a amusement park your friend danny

_____

_____

_____

_____

_____

_____

Score all words, group of numbers, or punctuation marks in these sentences as one point each, whether or not a correction is needed.

Score: _____ /41

seth nelson
105 garfield ave
madison wi 57293

my baby sister was born
on monday january 9
2006

carol asked where due the spoons forks and knifes go

_____

_____

_____

_____

you re garden has the prettier flowers of all my garden only has vegetables

_____

_____

_____

Weekly Assessment

Directions: Use your editing marks to make corrections on the sentence(s) below. Then rewrite the sentence(s) on the lines provided.

me and jack was siting around the house their aint nothing too do i said us could go sleding said jack yes what a great idea i shouted

Score all words, group of numbers, or punctuation marks in these sentences as one point each, whether or not a correction is needed.

Score: _____ /42

Name: _____   Date: _____

Unit 5 Assessment

Directions: Use your editing marks to make corrections on the sentence(s) below. Then rewrite the sentence(s) on the lines provided.

emmas too brothers jeff
and jeremy has bikes both
brothers bikes are blue jeff
and jeremy likes two race
with there bikes they has
even one some trophys

_____

_____

_____

_____

_____

Score all words, group of numbers, or punctuation marks in these sentences
as one point each, whether or not a correction is needed.

Score: _____ /36

1. The teacher said, "Happy New Year, everyone!"
2. "Are you older than your brother?" asked our neighbor, Mr. Smith.
3. We went on vacation to Daytona, Florida, in December.
4. "Don't you like to build lots of snowmen in the winter?" asked James.
5. My family and I were going to go to a play. My sister takes acting lessons, and she is in the play. "We need to leave in an hour to get there by 6:00!" shouted Dad.
6. Emily, why don't you ever come swimming with us anymore?
7. <u>Wintertime Fun</u> is a great book. I go to the library every Saturday to check out books.
8. Sally drew a picture of all her puppies and kitties.
9. Frank's favorite song is "America" by R. W. Fields.

10.
My Garden
I. Food
   A. Fruits
      1. strawberries
   B. Vegetables
      1. corn
II. Flowers
   A. Annuals
      1. sunflowers
   B. Perennials
      1. tulips

11. Yesterday Mom played golf, tennis, and basketball with Kim and me.
12. "No, I didn't catch a fish all day!" shouted Zach.
13. My dad flies airplanes, just like his best friend, Jake.
14. I made three wishes when I blew out my birthday candles.
15.
        2020 Greenview Ave.
        Atlanta, GA 72947
        January 15, 2006

Dear Rod,

    I'm having fun in San Francisco. We went to a zoo, an ocean beach, and an amusement park.

        Your friend,
        Danny

16. Seth Nelson
    105 Garfield Ave.
    Madison, WI 57293
17. My baby sister was born Monday, January 9, 2006.
18. Carol asked, "Where do the spoons, forks, and knives go?"
19. Your garden has the prettiest flowers of all. My garden only has vegetables.
20. Jack and I were sitting around the house. "There isn't anything to do," I said. "We could go sledding," said Jack. "Yes, what a great idea!" I shouted.

Unit 5 Assessment
Answer Key

emma's ~~too~~ *two* brothers, jeff and jeremy, ~~has~~ *have* bikes.

both brothers' bikes are blue. jeff and jeremy

likes *to* ~~two~~ race with ~~there~~ *their* bikes. they ~~has~~ *have* even

~~one~~ *won* some ~~trophys~~ *trophies*.

Emma's two brothers, Jeff and Jeremy, have bikes. Both brothers' bikes are blue. Jeff and Jeremy like to race with their bikes. They have even won some trophies.

bob said both are
neighbors swimming
pools is for foots deep

you're bed is softest then
mine but roxys bed is the
softer of all

well have to valentines
day partys on february
14 we had a christmas
party on december 20

i will right a poem called
friends too put on my
valentines said bonnie

Weekly Assessment

me and my friend we goed
too the market on
saturday us got some fruit
two take home us buyed
ate boxes of cherrys for
peachs and to apple

_____

_____

_____

_____

_____

_____

_____

*Score all words, group of numbers, or punctuation marks in these sentences
as one point each, whether or not a correction is needed.*

Score: _____ /34

is valentines day in
january february or
march asked jenny

alissa swimmed at the
pool all day on saturday
february 7

doesnt you wanna go
with us no more tim

my cousin carter and me
likes too read the book
titled to many
valentines

Weekly Assessment

Directions: Make an outline. (Title) emperor penguins (Main topics) habitat, appearance (Subtopics) South Pole, size, body coverings (Details) antarctica, ocean, biggest penguin, waterproof feathers.

_____

_____

_____

_____

_____

_____

_____

_____

_____

_____

Score all words, group of numbers, or punctuation marks in these sentences as one point each, whether or not a correction is needed.

Score: _____ /33

yes us has a knew puppy
named torii said seth
excitedly

aunt nicole she is really
nice said my friend
katie

the too childs saw a
elephant and a ape at
the zoo on sunday

jackie shouted happy
valentines day mrs
anderson

Weekly Assessment

Directions: Make corrections on the sentence(s) below. Then rewrite them on the lines.

595 eastside hwy trenton nj 13579
february 15 2006 dear joe us both
enjoyed watching your're basketball
game last friday knight were glad
the eagles one the game with love
grandma and grandpa

_____

_____

_____

_____

_____

_____

_____

Score: _____ /41

janet wilson
670 main st
raleigh nc 37345

do west schools classes
start at 800 asked mrs
bryan

no i aint gonna go too
grandview park today

me and aaron are
buddys and us likes too
go runing together

Weekly Assessment

Directions: Use your editing marks to make corrections on the sentence(s) below. Then rewrite the sentence(s) on the lines provided.

my friend jake has ate horses
him horses is brown black and
white there hoofs are the
larger ive ever seen i shouted
us rided jakes horses all day

_____

_____

_____

_____

_____

_____

_____

Score all words, group of numbers, or punctuation marks in these sentences
as one point each, whether or not a correction is needed.

Score: _____ /42

Unit 6 Assessment

Directions: Use your editing marks to make corrections on the sentence(s) below. Then rewrite the sentence(s) on the lines provided.

in march sues family is gonna go too orlando florida them will visit walt disney world and sea world theyll have sew much fun their i cant wait until next month sue said excitedly

_____

_____

_____

_____

_____

_____

Score all words, group of numbers, or punctuation marks in these sentences as one point each, whether or not a correction is needed.

Score: _____ /45

Unit 6
Answer Key

1. Bob said, "Both our neighbors' swimming pools are four feet deep."

2. Your bed is softer than mine, but Roxy's bed is the softest of all.

3. We'll have two Valentine's Day parties on February 14. We had a Christmas Party on December 20.

4. "I will write a poem called "Friends" to put on my Valentines," said Bonnie.

5. My friend and I went to the market on Saturday. We got some fruit to take home. We bought eight boxes of cherries, four peaches, and two apples.

6. "Is Valentine's Day in January, February, or March?" asked Jenny.

7. Alissa swam at the pool all day on Saturday, February 7.

8. Don't you want to go with us anymore, Tim?

9. My cousin, Carter, and I like to read the book <u>Too Many Valentines</u>.

10.
Emperor Penguins

I. Habitat

   A. South Pole

      1. Antarctica

      2. Ocean

II. Appearance

   A. Size

      1. Biggest penguin

   B. Body coverings

      1. Waterproof feathers

11. "Yes, we have a new puppy named Torii!" said Seth excitedly.

12. "Aunt Nicole is really nice," said my friend, Katie.

13. The two children saw an elephant and an ape at the zoo on Sunday.

14. Jackie shouted, "Happy Valentine's Day, Mrs. Anderson!"

15.
      595 Eastside Hwy.
      Trenton, NJ 13579
      February 15, 2006

Dear Joe,

    We both enjoyed watching your basketball game last Friday night. We're glad the Eagles won the game!

      With love,
      Grandma and Grandpa

16. Janet Wilson
    670 Main St.
    Raleigh, NC 37345

17. "Do West School's classes start at 8:00?" asked Mrs. Bryan.

18. No, I am not going to go to Grandview Park today.

19. Aaron and I are buddies, and we like to go running together.

20. My friend, Jake, has eight horses. His horses are brown, black, and white. "Their hooves are the largest I've ever seen!" I shouted. We rode Jake's horses all day.

Unit 6 Assessment
Answer Key

in march sue's family is ~~gonna~~ *going to* go *too* orlando, florida. ~~them~~ *They* will visit walt disney world and *see* *Sea* world. they'll have *sew* *so* much fun *their* *there* "i can't wait until next month!" sue said excitedly.

In March Sue's family is going to go to Orlando, Florida. They will visit Walt Disney World and Sea World. They'll have so much fun there. "I can't wait until next month!" Sue said excitedly.

me and her likes
shareing a bedroom said
ann

_____

_____

_____

_____

yesterday the boys plays
with there brother but
him didnt have no fun

_____

_____

_____

_____

toms brother jack he had
to dime for nickel and
ate penneys

march 1 2006 was the
day we leaved on are trip
too puerto rico

Weekly Assessment

Directions: Use your editing marks to make corrections on the sentence(s) below. Then rewrite the sentence(s) on the lines provided.

have you red the short story
called a rainbow its the goodest
st patricks day story ive ever red
the mans in the story finded the
gold at the end of the rainbow
and them lived happily ever after

_____

_____

_____

_____

_____

*Score all words, group of numbers, or punctuation marks in these sentences
as one point each, whether or not a correction is needed.*

Score: _____ /49

are cat fluffy is biger
then you re dog rex

me have teached third
grade four twenty years
said mr c s green

that movie runned from
700 too 900 last saturday
at the showtime theater

yes ive red the book titled
the shining shamrock by
jon blarney

Weekly Assessment

Directions: Make an outline. (Title) bats (Main topics) types, characteristics, habitats (Subtopics) fruit bat, vampire bat, nocturnal, echo location, caves, trees.

_____

_____

_____

_____

_____

_____

_____

_____

_____

_____

Score all words, group of numbers, or punctuation marks in these sentences as one point each, whether or not a correction is needed.

Score: _____ /31

is st patricks day on friday march 17 asked mario

their were a flock of gooses buy are house yesterday once i seen a flock of ducks in central park

due you has a orange
bike or a yellow bike
asked nick

martha she singed to
songs in east high
schools talent show

Weekly Assessment

Directions: Use your editing marks to make corrections on the sentence(s) below. Then rewrite the sentence(s) on the lines provided.

p o box 123 mesa ar 87502 march 5
2006 dear jan please come too my st
patricks day party on friday march 17
2006 at 700 dont forget two wear
green your friend erin

_____

_____

_____

_____

_____

_____

_____

_____

Score: _____ /50

eli davis
50 n brown blvd
ireland indiana 37244

mr sean fitzpatrick from
ireland said happy st
patricks day

is tara or emily shortest
asked my sisters friend
gina

my favorite season is
spring but i also likes
summer

Weekly Assessment

Directions: Use your editing marks to make corrections on the sentence(s) below. Then rewrite the sentence(s) on the lines provided.

the carsons are leaving on a trip them is gonna go two honolulu hawaii four too weaks dont forget too pack you're swiming suit said mom

Score all words, group of numbers, or punctuation marks in these sentences as one point each, whether or not a correction is needed.

Score: _____ /34

Name: _____ Date: _____

Unit 7 Assessment

Directions: Use your editing marks to make corrections on the sentence(s) below. Then rewrite the sentence(s) on the lines provided.

in february my friend rod move away i never sea him no more next summer are familys are planing on takeing a vacation too california together its gonna bee fun

_____

_____

_____

_____

_____

Score all words, group of numbers, or punctuation marks in these sentences as one point each, whether or not a correction is needed.

Score: _____ /37

1. "She and I like sharing a bedroom," said Ann.

2. Yesterday the boys played with their brother, but he didn't have any fun.

3. Tom's brother, Jack, had two dimes, four nickels, and eight pennies.

4. March 1, 2006, was the day we left on our trip to Puerto Rico.

5. Have you read the short story called "A Rainbow"? It's the best St. Patrick's Day story I've ever read. The men in the story found the gold at the end of the rainbow, and they lived happily ever after.

6. Our cat, Fluffy, is bigger than your dog, Rex.

7. "I have taught third grade for twenty years," said Mr. C. S. Green.

8. That movie ran from 7:00 to 9:00 last Saturday at the Showtime Theater.

9. Yes, I have read the book titled <u>The Shining Shamrock</u> by Jon Blarney.

10.

Bats

I. Types

A. Fruit bat

B. Vampire bat

II. Characteristics

A. Nocturnal

B. Echo location

III. Habitats

A. Caves

B. Trees

11. "Is St. Patrick's Day on Friday, March 17?" asked Mario.

12. There was a flock of geese by our house yesterday. Once I saw a flock of ducks in Central Park.

13. "Do you have an orange bike or a yellow bike?" asked Nick.

14. Martha sang two songs in East High School's talent show.

15.

P.O. Box 123
Mesa, AR 87502
March 5, 2006

Dear Jan,

    Please come to my St. Patrick's Day party on Friday, March 17, 2006, at 7:00. Don't forget to wear green!

Your friend,
Erin

16. Eli Davis
    50 N. Brown Blvd.
    Ireland, IN 37244

17. Mr. Sean Fitzpatrick from Ireland said, "Happy St. Patrick's Day!"

18. "Is Tara or Emily shorter?" asked my sister's friend, Gina.

19. My favorite season is spring, but I also like summer.

20. The Carsons are leaving on a trip. They are going to go to Honolulu, Hawaii, for two weeks. "Don't forget to pack your swimming suit," said Mom.

Unit 7 Assessment

Answer Key

in february my friend, rod, moved away. i never sea him no more. next summer our familys are planing on takeing a vacation too california together. it's gonna bee fun!

(edited to:)

In February my friend, Rod, moved away. I never see him anymore. Next summer our families are planning on taking a vacation to California together. It's going to be fun!

soccer is my favorite sport to shouted jimmy

there blew car runned well but it's paint was faded

does you likes to stay at
aunt mays house or aunt
julies

ouch i just got stinged
buy a be shouted jill

Weekly Assessment

Directions: Use your editing marks to make corrections on the sentence(s) below. Then rewrite the sentence(s) on the lines provided.

my to cousins molly and polly has for dogs there dogs is training too bee Seeing Eye dogs the for dogs harnesses is vary important four there training

_____

_____

_____

_____

_____

_____

_____

Score all words, group of numbers, or punctuation marks in these sentences as one point each, whether or not a correction is needed.

Score: _____ /34

will easter bee in april
this year asked the
twins sister megan

are countrys name is the
united states of america

sherry will meet me and
chris at willow tree
mall too go shoping

sam asked didnt you get
no candy in youre easter
basket

Weekly Assessment

Directions: Make an outline. (Title) great white shark (Main topics) description, habitat
(Subtopics) size, color, shorelines (Details) length, weight, white and gray, temperate climates.

_____

_____

_____

_____

_____

_____

_____

_____

_____

_____

_____

_____

*Score all words, group of numbers, or punctuation marks in these sentences
as one point each, whether or not a correction is needed.*

Score: _____ /33

you're dog fred shouldnt
chew on it's leash said
dad

that s the harder
homework are teacher
mr petersen have ever
given too us

are teacher she red too
us from a magic tree
house book on thursday

_____

_____

_____

_____

_____

my little sister she
yelled gimme that toy
write now

_____

_____

_____

_____

Weekly Assessment

Directions: Use your editing marks to make corrections on the sentence(s) below. Then rewrite the sentence(s) on the lines provided.

1001 broadway ave charleston sc 14793 april 15 2006 dear aunt sue were haveing a vary nice time in south carolina i wish you were hear with us your niece isabel

Score all words, group of numbers, or punctuation marks in these sentences as one point each, whether or not a correction is needed.

Score: _____ /39

jan olson
700 state st
atlanta georgia 45678

---

alan has to guinea pigs
three mouses and won
gerbil as pets

hurry we will bee leaving
in a hour said mom

amy writed a poem
called springtime her
took it home and red it
too her family

Weekly Assessment

Directions: Use your editing marks to make corrections on the sentence(s) below. Then rewrite the sentence(s) on the lines provided.

tim whats you're favorite
subject in school asked
dad me and my friend
nate likes math the best
answered tim i do to
shouted tims sister robin

_____

_____

_____

_____

_____

Score all words, group of numbers, or punctuation marks in these sentences as one point each, whether or not a correction is needed.

Score: _____ /46

Unit 8 Assessment

Directions: Use your editing marks to make corrections on the sentence(s) below. Then rewrite the sentence(s) on the lines provided.

brian and me were watching are
favorite show called superheroes
on television its on every friday
knight at 800 this is a great
show said brian yes i really like
it to i said

_____

_____

_____

_____

_____

_____

_____

Score: _____ /50

1. "Soccer is my favorite sport, too!" shouted Jimmy.

2. Their blue car ran well, but its paint was faded.

3. Do you like to stay at Aunt May's house or Aunt Julie's?

4. "Ouch, I just got stung by a bee!" shouted Jill.

5. My two cousins, Molly and Polly, have four dogs. Their dogs are training to be Seeing Eye dogs. The four dogs' harnesses are very important for their training.

6. "Will Easter be in April this year?" asked the twins' sister, Megan.

7. Our country's name is the United States of America.

8. Sherry will meet Chris and me at Willow Tree Mall to go shopping.

9. Sam asked, "Didn't you get any candy in your Easter basket?"

10.

Great White Shark

   I.   Description

       A. Size

           1. Length

           2. Weight

       B. Color

           1. White and gray

   II. Habitat

       A. Shorelines

           1. Temperate climates

11. "Your dog, Fred, shouldn't chew on its leash," said Dad.

12. That's the hardest homework our teacher, Mr. Petersen, has ever given to us!

13. Our teacher read to us from a <u>Magic Tree House</u> book on Thursday.

14. My little sister yelled, "Give me that toy right now!"

15.

1001 Broadway Ave.
Charleston, SC 14793
April 15, 2006

Dear Aunt Sue,

   We're having a very nice time in South Carolina. I wish you were here with us!

Your niece,
Isabel

16. Jan Olson
    700 State St.
    Atlanta, Georgia 45678

17. Alan has two guinea pigs, three mice, and one gerbil as pets.

18. "Hurry, we will be leaving in an hour!" said Mom.

19. Amy wrote a poem called "Springtime." She took it home and read it to her family.

20. "Tim, what's your favorite subject in school?" asked Dad. "My friend, Nate, and I like math the best," answered Tim. "I do, too!" shouted Tim's sister, Robin.

Unit 8 Assessment
<u>Answer Key</u>

brian and me were watching are favorite show, superheroes, on television. it's on every friday knight at 8:00. "this is a great show!" said brian. "yes, i really like it, too!" i said.

Brian and I were watching our favorite show, called <u>Superheroes,</u> on television. It's on every Friday night at 8:00. "This is a great show!" said Brian. "Yes, I really like it, too!" I said.

Cumulative Assessment

Name: _____ Date: _____ Score: _____

Directions: Correct each sentence. Use editing marks.

1. her takes care of to dog five calfs and seven bunnys on there farm

_____

_____

(See Unit 1 Answer Key, page 24, #12, for answer.)

2. me and my best friend went too a concert at 300 last thursday september 8

_____

_____

(See Unit 1 Answer Key, page 25, #16, for answer.)

3. jim baker 39 rolling rd duluth mn 56780

_____

_____

_____

(See Unit 1 Answer Key, page 25, #19, for answer.)

4. me and pam buyed too pumpkins four halloween said meg

_____

_____

(See Unit 2 Answer Key, page 43, #3, for answer.)

5. im gonna have a apple and a orange four a snack

_____

_____

(See Unit 2 Answer Key, page 43, #7, for answer.)

6. all the neighbors houses on pine street was painted white

_____

_____

(See Unit 2 Answer Key, page 43, #8, for answer.)

Cumulative Assessment *(cont.)*

7. my favorite poem is fall by b j white

_____

_____

(See Unit 3 Answer Key, page 60, #11, for answer.)

8. those to mouses are gray once we catched a mouse

_____

_____

(See Unit 3 Answer Key, page 61, #18, for answer.)

9. that boy he is hurt to shouted chris

_____

_____

(See Unit 4 Answer Key, page 77, #1, for answer.)

10. is you tallest then you're brother kasey asked

_____

_____

(See Unit 4 Answer Key, page 77, #4, for answer.)

11. that dogs tail is the longer of all said ken

_____

_____

(See Unit 4 Answer Key, page 77, #6, for answer.)

12. the childrens dentist dr davis cleaned there tooths on wednesday

_____

_____

(See Unit 4 Answer Key, page 78, #17, for answer.)

Cumulative Assessment *(cont.)*

13. yesterday mom play golf tennis and basketball with I and kim

_____

_____

(See Unit 5 Answer Key, page 92, #11, for answer.)

14. carol asked where due the spoons forks and knifes go

_____

_____

(See Unit 5 Answer Key, page 93, #18, for answer.)

15. you're bed is softest then mine but roxys bed is the softer of all

_____

_____

(See Unit 6 Answer Key, page 107, #2, for answer.)

16. yes ive red the book titled the shining shamrock by jon blarney

_____

_____

(See Unit 7 Answer Key, page 122, #9, for answer.)

17. sam asked didnt you get no candy in you're easter basket

_____

_____

(See Unit 8 Answer Key, page 137, #9, for answer.)

18. hurry we will bee leaving in a hour said mom

_____

_____

(See Unit 8 Answer Key, page 138, #18, for answer.)

Cumulative Assessment *(cont.)*

19.

2020 greenview ave
atlanta ga 72947
january 15 2006

dear rod

im having fun in san francisco us goed too a zoo a ocean beach and a amusement park

your friend
danny

_____

_____

_____

_____

_____

_____

_____

_____

(See Unit 5 Answer Key, page 92, #15, for answer.)

Cumulative Assessment *(cont.)*

20. Use the following information to make an outline: (Title) my garden (Main topics) food, flowers, (Subtopics) fruits, vegetables, annuals, perennials (Details) strawberries, corn, sunflowers, tulips

_____

_____

_____

_____

_____

_____

_____

_____

_____

_____

_____

_____

_____

(See Unit 5 Answer Key, page 92, #10, for answer.)

Blank Writing Form

Name: _____ Date: _____

_____

_____

_____

_____

_____

_____

Name: _____ Date: _____

_____

_____

_____

_____

_____